"This guide is an essential companion for the journey a new pastor must make and the challenges he will face in his first few critical months. It's a comprehensive, solidly-researched and practical resource that helps a new pastor to build strong relationships with staff and parishioners and thereby increase his own effectiveness."

—H. Richard McCord, former Executive Director of the U.S. Bishops' Secretariat of Laity, Marriage, Family Life and Youth

"Serving a faith community as its pastor is not like any other job. Transitions between pastoral assignments come with some unique challenges. Built on a strong biblical foundation, this guide offers practical strategies to help priests make that transition, whether for the first time or the fifth. This helpful and easy-to-read book should be handed out with letters announcing new assignments."

—Mary Elizabeth Sperry, author *Scripture in the Parish: A Guide for Catholic Ministry*

Navigating Pastoral Transitions

A Priest's Guide

Edited by
Graziano Marcheschi

LITURGICAL PRESS
Collegeville, Minnesota

www.litpress.org

1   2   3   4   5   6   7   8   9

Library of Congress Cataloging-in-Publication Data

Navigating pastoral transitions : a priest's guide / edited by Graziano Marcheschi.
    pages cm
   Includes bibliographical references.
   ISBN 978-0-8146-3805-7 — ISBN 978-0-8146-3830-9 (ebook)
   1. Catholic Church—Clergy—Relocation.   I. Marcheschi, Graziano, editor of compilation.

BX1912.N38   2013
253'2—dc23   2013019768

Contents

Preface

The Archdiocese of Chicago and Loyola University Chicago funded this guide through a grant from the Lilly Endowment, Inc. *Sustaining Pastoral Excellence* (SPE) program. Dedicated to finding and sustaining excellent pastoral work in several U.S. Christian denominations, SPE helped the Archdiocese and University found INSPIRE. The INSPIRE project promotes pastoral excellence in parishes of the Archdiocese. Its acronym summarizes its mission: to Identify, Nurture, and Sustain Pastoral Imagination through Resources for Excellence. Serving parish staffs throughout the Archdiocese, INSPIRE helps them develop collaborative expressions of excellence in pastoral leadership.

On behalf of the Archdiocese of Chicago Department of Personnel Services, the Office for Lay Ecclesial Ministry submitted a proposal to INSPIRE recommending a Pastor Transition Study Team to explore the challenges and opportunities inherent in pastor transitions. The task force formed the following question to express their singular mandate: Can we find better ways for priests to make their way to new parishes as pastors?

Subsequently the quest was extended to see how parish staff and parishioner leaders can best work through this difficult time in the life of the parish, and booklets were developed for these groups.

Members of the Study Team designed and implemented surveys of pastors, parish staffs, and parishioner leaders in the Archdiocese of Chicago who had recently experienced a pastor change. The team is grateful for the participation of ordained and lay leaders who generously contributed their observations and insights.

The following persons contributed time and effort to the Archdiocese of Chicago Pastor Transitions Study Team:

Rev. Michael Ahlstrom, Vicar for the Diaconate Community
Mark Bersano, Assistant Director, INSPIRE
Ralph Bonaccorsi, Office of Conciliation
Rev. John Clemens, Pastor, Our Lady of Hope
Rev. James Donovan, Secretary, Priest Placement Board
Rev. Vincent Costello, Co-Vicar for Priests
Daniel Gast, Director, INSPIRE
Rita Kattner, DMin, Office for Councils,
     Christ Renews His Parish
Kathleen Leggdas, Director, Office of Ministerial Evaluation
Kevin O'Connor, INSPIRE Facilitator,
     Loyola University Chicago
Carol Walters, Director, Lay Ecclesial Ministry
Cathy Walz, Office for Catechesis and Youth

Commissioned Editor:
Graziano Marcheschi, DMin, Executive Director of
     University Ministry, Saint Xavier University

Clergy quotes used in this guide were selected from responses to a survey sent to priests in the Archdiocese of Chicago who assumed new pastorates in 2006 and 2007. Some questions asked of the newly appointed pastors included:

> **"How was your last move?" "What worked well?"**
> A sample response was: "Meeting with the staff and organizations of the parish I was assigned to prior to the move. Getting a feel for the 'lay of the land' before actually moving in. The time between the notification and arrival was beneficial for transition."

> **"What would you change?" "What would you make certain to do again?"** A sample response was: "I certainly would have set up some process to deal with people's fears. People wanted to keep holding on to me

till I left. It was hard. I wish I had taken the initiative to invite discussion and encourage openness."

Using these insights and responses, *A Priest's Guide* aims to help priests—whether first-time pastors or veterans—understand the dynamics of pastoral transition and to prepare better for change.

Introduction

To change or not to change? That is the question facing any priest who receives an assignment—welcomed or not—to shepherd a new parish.

Transition evokes a wide array of emotions and requires adjustment from everyone involved. There are no shortcuts. The transition process must work at its own pace.

> Be strong and steadfast; have no fear or dread . . . , for it is the LORD, your God, who marches with you; he will never fail you or forsake you.
> *(Deut 31:6)*
>
> So whoever is in Christ is a new creation: the old things have passed away; behold, new things have come.
> *(2 Cor 5:17)*

Perhaps you've heard the ecclesial admonition to "Change nothing the first year." While that axiom may not be absolute, especially in cases of abuse or fraudulent practices or structural building problems, it provides a helpful reminder that a new pastor needs to move slowly in making changes. A more realistic version of this adage might be "Change nothing within the first 120 days."

Either way, you don't want to ignore the wisdom of that counsel. Your tools for the transition are conversation, observation, inquiry, and empathic listening. As parishioners and staff come to accept a new pastor and he in turn comes to understand the parish's history and current situation, mutual trust begins to grow and openness to change increases.

1

The reality is that staff and parishioners *expect* change. They know they would be naïve to think otherwise. Everyone wants change that's beneficial and that results from genuine consultation. But how do you make change that is beneficial and consultative?

Accentuate the Positive, Adjust to the Negative

All change creates stress; some change also poses significant challenges. However, the process of transitioning "from" and transitioning "to" is also charged with new possibilities that inspire hope. At any given moment when you are anticipating a major change, you might find yourself focusing on the possibilities or on the anxiety. Often, you may feel you have little or no control over which emotion takes hold of you.

Changing jobs and moving to a new home are widely experienced changes. Sometimes they occur independently, sometimes together. You can readily acknowledge the inherent stresses in those transitions. But some moves, as you may know well, are harder than others.

Prior to relocating, a friend commented that he didn't mind moving to a new home. This man was married and moving to a new neighborhood, and his family moved with him; his job didn't change, and he made the move voluntarily, so his new circumstances were not radically different from his former circumstances. He experienced minor stress related to managing the logistical details of the physical move from one home to another.

Priests, on the other hand, move under very different circumstances. They experience multiple stressors that seem to converge all at once, resulting in a distinct set of challenges. Transition can be as positive an experience for clergy as for anyone, but it can also be disruptive and difficult in ways that are unique to priests' lifestyle and circumstances.

Some priests may not point to the physical change itself, but to the necessary adjustments that must occur during the change that account for the anxiety, discomfort, anger, and even the wild anticipation priests sometimes experience. Much of this discomfort seems to occur during the liminal "in-between" time as priests anticipate leaving their old parishes and prepare for moving to new ones.

The Goal of A Priest's Guide

This resource seeks to help you with the significant transition you are approaching. The Archdiocese of Chicago—where this guide claims it roots—has well-developed policies and procedures for appointing pastors. For instance, Chicago's archdiocesan policy mandates that first-time pastors attend a New Pastor Workshop offered through the University of St. Mary of the Lake (ongoingformation@usml.edu). Nevertheless, pastors asked for help navigating the spiritual, psychological, and interpersonal aspects of transitioning from one parish to another.

In the following pages you will find ideas and resources for this critical time in your life. You are certainly well aware that while it is the individual priest who transitions, the staff and parish are also deeply impacted when a pastor leaves and a new pastor is appointed.

This guide, created for new and veteran pastors, is specifically designed to assist you and your parish in discovering the blessings and negotiating the challenges of the transition itself. It is the lead guide in a trio of resources that includes guides written for parish staff and for parishioners.

As supplemental resources, the three books of the *Navigating Pastoral Transitions* series are not intended to replace the policies and procedures of your own diocese or archdiocese. Links to many such documents are provided at www.litpress.org/pastoraltransitions /resources.

Recognizing Life-giving Choices

A Priest's Guide assumes God's active, loving, and transforming presence in all of life's transitions. It also assumes that your partnership with God and God's people leads to life-giving choices that help ensure successful transitions in any setting—particularly ministry. Cognizant of the critical time you are approaching, you are invited to take a prayerful, proactive stance toward your upcoming transition.

> In contrast, the fruit of the Spirit is love, joy, peace, patience, kindness, generosity, faithfulness, gentleness, self-control. Against such there is no law.   *(Gal 5:22-23)*

As you reflect on these materials and dialogue with respected and trusted individuals (fellow priest, spiritual director, friend), you may begin to recognize this time of transition as an opportunity for renewed engagement in life, renewed vision of your ministry, and for greater openness to the new. At this moment you could easily narrow your focus to the "physical move," but you may instead come to recognize that change can be redemptive.

May you be blessed with the latter!

Part One

The Pastor and Transition

The Spiritual Dimensions

The paschal mystery is the heart of Christian spirituality. The dying and rising of Jesus is the model for your own daily experiences of death and resurrection. Transitioning to a new pastorate certainly qualifies as an opportunity for dying and rising.

This notion of dying and rising is intimately connected to the biblical notions of "call" and "journey." Those major themes, found throughout the Bible, are first encountered in the story of Abraham. His call to leave his people, his land, and his livelihood provides a clear paradigm for the pastoral transition priests face today. The Exodus story provides another paradigm and the gospels consistently characterize the life of Jesus as a journey undertaken in response to the call of the Father. These archetypes offer pastors in transition helpful models of faith, courage, and single-mindedness.

You are steeped in a culture that places its highest value on self-determination and personal fulfillment. But the Gospel says otherwise—that life is not all about you; God is the true center of your being. You are in the world but not of the world. In biblical language, it comes down to the difference between living in the flesh and living in the spirit, of surrendering to God's call rather than fulfilling purely personal desires.

As a priest, you understand well the meaning of "call." Your early subjective attraction to the life of a parish priest was made objective through the scrutiny of the seminary system and the call of the bishop on the day of ordination. A priest's very identity is one of being called and sent. But today the calling and sending of priests as pastors is more complicated than ever.

Using Scripture to Understand Your Call

For many years, the Chicago Archdiocese experienced an abundance of priests applying to be pastors, with several men often applying for the same parish. A priest sought a parish that seemed to be a good fit for him and then he submitted his application, presenting himself to the placement board as a worthy candidate.

That pattern has shifted because of the significantly lower number of active priests. Not so long ago, a priest wouldn't *qualify* for a pastorate unless he had been ordained for at least ten, fifteen, even twenty years. Now priests can be invited to become pastors as soon as a few years after ordination. Early calls to the duties of pastor place great challenges before young men who are still adjusting to priesthood. This new situation conjures the "call" experience of some of the biblical prophets. Like them, priests, with their unique strengths, weaknesses, interests, and preferences, are sometimes asked to go places they never intended to go, at least so early in their ministerial careers.

A priest facing a new assignment might open the Lectionary to the special Masses for vocations to priesthood and religious life and use the numerous Scripture passages found there as possible springboards for prayer. As you read the Bible, you might want to begin identifying any passages that you think speak directly to you during this time of transition. Several Scripture passages that might help a pastor in transition include:

During the garden agony Jesus asks that his pain be taken away. His ultimate prayer, however, is "Not my will, but yours be done" (Luke 22:42). The life of a priest mirrors that of Christ, subjecting his will to the will of the Father.

After giving Peter his "new assignment" to care for the sheep, Jesus concludes very pointedly, "'I say to you, when you were younger, you used to dress yourself and go where you wanted; but when you grow old, you will stretch out your hands, and someone else will dress you and lead you where you do not want to go.' He said this signifying by what kind of death he would glorify God. And when he had said this, he said to him, 'Follow me'" (John 21:18-19).

Jesus speaks those same words to each priest not only on his ordination day but constantly throughout his ministry and especially at those moments that are most characteristically Christian—when, like an aerialist, you have let go of one trapeze and hang in midair, waiting to catch the other as it swings toward you from the opposite side.

Moving into the Second Half of Life

Regardless of the age at which a priest becomes a pastor, and no matter whether it is his first or third pastorate, the experience of transition triggers a number of interior movements that are worth considering. The contemporary spiritual masters Ronald Rolheiser, OMI, and Richard Rohr, OFM, have done significant research on male spirituality. Most men, they say, spend the first half of life building up a healthy self-esteem and meeting needs for intimacy and generativity. During this time, their spiritual lives may be characterized as "wrestling with the devil," according to Rohr. The challenges include setting of boundaries and finding balance. Many young priests, who, like Martha, find themselves busy "about many things," might readily identify with the need to set boundaries and establish balance in their lives.

Significant loss usually triggers movement into the second half of the spiritual life. The death of a loved one, wounded pride, a health crisis, or a career disappointment are among the losses that can cause one's life to begin moving in a different direction. For some men, the rest of life becomes a process of shifting priorities. They may realize that much of what they once strove for or achieved does not really mean that much. They begin letting go. Now, they are no longer wrestling with the devil but with God (a much harder match, reported a senior priest). Instead of hoping to win, as against the devil, these men now hope to lose. They recall Mary listening at the feet of Jesus rather than Martha taking care of business. Often, the second half of the spiritual life does not begin until well after the biological second half of life has begun.[1]

> We were indeed buried with him through baptism into death, so that, just as Christ was raised from the dead by the glory of the Father, we too might live in newness of life.
> *(Rom 6:4)*

Pastors in transition, especially those in midlife or later, may wrestle with these kinds of issues. While younger priests may still be about fulfilling generativity needs when they become new pastors, they too eventually will enter this new stage and confront a new set of issues. A spiritual director is essential for men of any age to discern and negotiate the path the Lord is taking them on.

A recently appointed pastor commented on what helped him during his transition: "Strong relationship with Jesus Christ, support from my family, the Art of Pastoring Workshops through the Office for Ongoing Formation of Priests at USML . . . and I belong to a fraternity and have taken the vows of poverty, chastity and obedience."

Perhaps these thoughts will provoke further reflection and conversations with trusted guides who can help you maintain a healthy and desirable balance in the days ahead.

The Need for Conversation

To better negotiate the challenges of a new appointment, you will find it helpful to understand some of the psychological dimensions of transition and to keep in mind that a change of pastors affects:

- the pastor himself,
- the parish staff and leadership,
- the parishioners at large.

It can be mutually helpful to share with these other groups some conversations that could be planned and others that are spontaneous. Again, your spiritual director can be a great resource to help you anticipate or plan such encounters. Note that such helpful conversations can ideally take place both in the community you are preparing to leave and in the new parish you are joining. In all the settings where planned conversations may occur, you may want to recruit a skilled person to serve as facilitator.

As pastor, you will want and need to read the other two guides—for parish staff and for parish leaders—in *Navigating Pastoral Transitions* so that you can plan these conversations and understand the dynamics of change and transition for other members of the parish.

Notes

1. See Richard Rohr's book, *Falling Upward: A Spirituality for the Two Halves of Life* (San Francisco: Jossey-Bass, 2011), or search YouTube for one of his lectures about the two halves of life. Ronald Rolheiser treats related themes in *The Holy Longing: The Search for a Christian Spirituality* (New York: Doubleday, 1999) .

Mapping a Transition

It is important to clarify the difference between change and transition. Some researchers speak of change as a shift in the *external* situation. In that view, transition is the *internal reorientation* one goes through in response to external change. It's not change itself that you may fear, but the transition—the necessary interior adjustment with its array of emotions and stages.

William Bridges, who writes extensively about organizational and personal change, inverts the "beginning, middle, end" scenario and posits instead an "end, middle ground, beginning" construct:

Endings: This is the departure phase of saying good-bye, leave-taking, and letting go of what was.

Neutral Zone: This is the in-between phase of experiencing the liminality of needing to leave where you are but not yet identifying with where you are going. Though projects remain and responsibilities linger, as pastor you need to set up a timetable for how to wean yourself from your various involvements at the parish you are leaving.

New Beginnings: This is the reentry phase of adjusting to new surroundings and making them "home," the time when you embrace a new role and new relationships.[1]

The Stages of Transition in Action

See what three priests had to say about their experiences in these stages:

Endings

"I talked about 'Transition' and *my* transition at least two years before I left. I talked with parishioners, staff, spiritual director, and friends about it. It was no surprise to anyone."

Neutral Zone

"(One of the hard parts of the transition was) the fact that I was still focused on projects at St. _____ till the day I left. I was trying to organize a church renovation team before leaving, to make it easier on my successor."

New Beginnings

"When people ask me how the new place is, I tell them it is new—new faces, names, routines, facilities, staff, etc., etc. It is all difficult because it is new. I was comfortable, content, and pleased with where I was. I walked away from that into something completely new. That is difficult, it is also energizing, but it is all new."

The Land of Promise

The Exodus story illustrates the three-stage process. Israel left the land of Egypt and so left behind much of its identity. The people entered the in-between place of the desert where they were sorely tempted to return to the fleshpots of Egypt and the familiarity and predictability of their former lives. In that middle ground, however, they learned adaptive skills, and they shared visions of how things could be in a new place. Finally, they reached the Promised Land but even so, approached warily. Only after additional years of wandering in the "in-between" wilderness did they finally claim the land of promise.

This model can be readily applied to a priest's move from one parish to another, but it only goes so far. Stages one and three are predictable and assured: you will leave and you will enter the new assignment. What's unpredictable is that middle phase. It will be critically important to go there, bring others there, and stay there longer than you or anyone is likely to want. Think of middle ground as a time and place for rehearsal, testing, evaluating. There everyone can try new ways of working, and, because it's only "middle ground," the cost of failures or merely partial successes is relatively low.

Both external circumstances and interior disposition can hinder a productive experience of liminality, that time when you are between homes and can find your true home only in the hands of God. Priests who experience a longer period between being informed of their new assignment and making the actual move benefit significantly. It will be up to the individual priest to ensure that the intervening months provide opportunities to do the interior work that will enable him to approach the new "land" without the fear that beset Israelites for so many years.

Because this liminal period is critical, a priest must balance the responsibility of continuing to pastor his old parish with the need to prepare spiritually and psychologically to pastor a new one. It is essential that a priest take time to reflect on his departure. This includes grieving what will be left behind. A priest might easily ignore his feelings of loss, but if he fails to process his grief, unresolved feelings may surface in the new setting and take shape in his making unfavorable comparisons and perhaps even expressing hostility.

Other Stressors

The high level of stress inherent in transition can be exacerbated by many factors. If a newly appointed pastor is also a first-time pastor, the process is complicated by the transition to a new role as well as to a new parish. Leaving an assignment where he was particularly happy adds, of course, to the sense of loss.

Sometimes when a priest enters a parish where the previous pastor was dearly loved, the new pastor may encounter resentment simply because he is not the former pastor. If his leadership style differs noticeably from his predecessor's, the adjustment to this new pastorate can become all the more difficult. Even if the previous pastor was not popular, the new pastor may need significant time to gain parishioners' confidence.

Because he is now an "authority figure," a *first-time* pastor may feel disoriented in his new role. As an associate pastor, he may have been viewed more like one of the parishioners, or as a peer with staff. Now, as pastor, he may find people don't approach him as easily. Sometimes he may feel treated as an adversary. During transition, especially for a first-time pastor who is recently ordained, maintaining close relationships with a mentor, the local dean, and one's bishop or episcopal vicar can ease adjustment to the new role.

> Regarding the importance of taking the necessary time, one priest surveyed suggested: "Listen. Listen. Listen! Take your time on ANY changes (you make). People don't like changes."

Social scientists say that among the most significant stressors in life are death of a loved one, divorce, moving from one's residence, and changing jobs. When a priest changes assignments, he is dealing with stressors that in analogous ways mimic these life changes.

Insights from the Stages of Grieving

The groundbreaking work of the late psychiatrist Elizabeth Kübler-Ross, a pioneer on death and dying, regarding the stages of grieving offers insight into the transition process priests undergo when they become pastors or move from one pastorate to another. Using the stages of grieving as a construct for pastoral transition, you can see how stressors experienced under different circumstances can resemble those experienced in pastor transition. As with the population addressed by Kübler-Ross, priests going through transition may not experience the grief steps in this typical sequence. Very likely priests will experience movements back and forth among the stages, and tidiness of the grieving process and straight-line progression are extremely rare.

Using Kübler-Ross's stages of grieving as a model for behavior, you might experience these emotions during your transition period:

Denial: Initially a priest might set aside or bury his emotions regarding the stress of both leaving a beloved assignment and adjusting to a new role in a new parish. It will eventually catch up with him. As one priest observed, "Not taking sufficient time to mourn leaving my previous assignment and not being patient enough to transition into the new environment made (my) transition difficult."

Anger: Some priests may feel bitter about a change they did not really anticipate or want. The new parish may not be at all what they expected. They may be angry about having to deal with the challenges of adjusting to the new situation or the resistance they may be encountering. One priest in the survey expressed his anger, saying, "The archdiocese was not forthright with information regarding the parish. They *wanted* me to come here."

Bargaining: In the Kübler-Ross construct, "bargaining" is usually understood to be a person's *quid pro quo* with God: "Heal me or my loved one and I'll do xyz." Though it's not the same as dealing with illness or death, pastoral transition can bring about the same kind of bargaining. A priest may accept the reality of his change but in a limited and conditional way. To hold on to the life he had before, he may dwell on an endless series of "what ifs," or even attempt to "play the system" in order to extend his current tenure.

Depression and Resignation: Sometimes a priest can be resigned to face the inevitable while still lacking interior assent to make the move. He lacks a sense of hope or joy about the change and instead lingers in sadness, believing his life will never be quite the same. He may settle in and try to adjust, but he can't claim to be altogether happy. This very common stage may be brief, or it may linger for some time. Priests speak especially of the difficulty of moving on at an older age when they feel settled and have less energy to face the challenges of building new relationships and negotiating the new personalities that await them. Whatever the context, this is a time when it's important to resist the temptation to "take care of it myself" and instead talk about your feelings and the situation with a trusted listener.

Acceptance: Most pastors work through the emotions of the prior four stages and come to accept and adjust to their new parish and their new role. Psychology and self-help efforts, however, won't be enough to reach acceptance. It is essential that a priest utilize the spiritual resources of a healthy prayer life, a spiritual director, and a pastor mentor. The importance of these elements should not be underestimated. Without them, a pastor may soon find himself alone in a desert of discontent (see the stage above). When a priest finally arrives at acceptance, it's a great time for him to assess the new ground and ask, "What new work (or play, or ministry) can I do here that I didn't get to do before?" Ultimately, transitions that are well managed bring one a sense of renewal and achievement, and even a sense of finding new life and resurrection! Who wouldn't want that?

It is good to give yourself permission to take the long view. The process of transition may take anywhere from one to three years. Though the steps mentioned above comprise a normal part of the transition process, it remains important throughout the transition for you to engage in self-reflection and seek self-knowledge. During stressful periods, you may be tempted to seek comfort in behaviors inconsistent with a priestly lifestyle. To avoid

> What I do, I do not understand. For I do not do what I want, but I do what I hate. *(Rom 7:15)*

such dangers, you would be wise to consciously choose behaviors that typify your best self and are most characteristic of a healthy priestly life.

Notes

1. William Bridges, *Managing Transitions: Making the Most of Change*, 3rd ed. (Cambridge, MA: Da Capo Lifelong Books, 2009).

Part Two

The Pastor and Parish Staff in Transition

Strategies for Entering a New Parish

The Give and Take of Transition

As with any workplace and living situation, there is a lot of "give and take" to consider and implement, some that is immediate in nature and some that comes with a bit of study and planning.

A pastor in a new parish assignment must deal with not only a new workplace but also, in most cases, a new living situation, whether on the parish site or nearby. And, most important, the new pastor must figure out how to relate to all the people involved in a transition—and there are many!

A wise practice when coming into a new parish is to learn whether people have ministerial role descriptions, to review these, and then learn peoples' perceptions about what is written about their roles. This certainly applies to the ordained members of the pastoral team as well as to the lay parish staff. Before discussing pastoral roles and responsibilities with anyone, you might consult your diocese for guidelines for any of these roles. Some dioceses may provide template statements to help clarify expectations for the pastor emeritus, the associate pastor, and the deacon.

Rectory Life

Moving to a new rectory often means entering a very different living situation. The new pastor may be the only priest, or the only full-time priest, in the house. On the other hand, the new pastor may find that for the first time in years he is living with an associate pastor (or in a rare case, even two), or a resident priest, or a retired priest who may be his predecessor, or some combination of these priests. If there *are* other priests in the house, it will probably take some time for the group to adjust to living with someone new in the rectory, especially if the group's time together is significant.

However, since priests often see and know things other staff members do not, the men the new pastor inherits can be great resources for helping to understand the history of the community, who the major players are, and where the land mines that every parish has are buried. If the incoming pastor has specific expectations about life in the rectory (such as eating dinner together on certain nights), he should discuss these expectations with his housemates as early as possible and invite them to share their ideas about the living situation.

Relating to Current Ordained Staff

Some specific situations involving current ordained staff may include:

Resident Priest Emeritus: Often when a new pastor is appointed, his recently retired predecessor, or another senior priest, may also be living in the parish house. The attitude with which each priest approaches the new living situation will determine whether the retiring pastor's or senior priest's presence will be a blessing or a challenge for the new pastor. If the former pastor truly intends to step back from being in charge, and makes this explicit when people come to him with requests or complaints, the situation will be a blessing for the new pastor. If the new pastor is hospitable and affirming of his predecessor and invites him to share his wisdom as well as to continue ministering, the blessing for both priests and for the parishioners will be magnified.

Deacons: Many parishes enjoy the ministry of a deacon assigned to them by the bishop. There may even be two or more deacons who serve in the parish. Usually, the deacon can be a valuable asset to the new pastor during his transition period of coming to know and adjust to the new parish. The deacon occupies a unique place in the parish, and, if a longtime parishioner, is able to offer dual perspectives as parishioner and fellow clergyman. Sometimes parishioners feel more comfortable expressing their concerns to a deacon rather than to the pastor, so that the deacon becomes a go-between for communication and an important ally to the pastor.

If a new pastor has never ministered alongside a deacon, he should be aware of the need for clear and sensitive communications with his deacon(s). Because deacons are often part-time volunteers, they can be easily overlooked by the pastor and parish staff. In some cases, staff members may resent the deacon because they do not understand or appreciate the diaconal role or there may be a history that left scarred relationships. The new pastor should be attentive to such tensions and ensure there is adequate and effective communication to help avoid conflict.

Relating to the Previous Pastor

The previous pastor can be your best source of support in your transition as new pastor of the parish he once shepherded. Or, he can be the source of great discontent—yours and others'—if the relationship between him and you as the new shepherd of his former parish is not addressed.

Some Chicago pastors reported that pre-arrival meetings with a pastor-less staff were mutually beneficial, yielding insight for the pastor-elect and much needed assurance to the staff. It is often the case that staff persons put program or pastoral initiatives "on hold" until the new pastor arrives. It can be helpful to assess with them the wisdom of that practice if several weeks remain until you take up the new leader role.

Some helpful tips for working with the previous pastor and establishing yourself as the new shepherd in town include:

Meet early in the process with the current pastor. Then continue meeting with him throughout the transition period to create opportunities for communication and clarification of questions.

Understand your feelings about the transition. Both current and incoming pastors must be aware of and deal effectively with their emotions. The departing pastor may recognize it is time to move on, but he may feel guilty about leaving the parish. The incoming pastor may feel anxious about the unknown, wondering if this parish will be a good match and if his personality and skills will fit. Both incoming and outgoing pastors typically experience parallel concerns regarding loss of friends, community, and neighborhood, and about loneliness, acceptance, and whether they have the energy to begin again.

Discuss with the outgoing pastor details of the transition process. You will want to clarify together how to handle announcements, liturgies, personnel concerns, finances, plant maintenance, community involvement and outreach, and so on.

Set dates. Each time you and the current pastor meet, set the date for your next meeting. This way you will protect the date and avoid the nuisance of telephone tag.

Appreciate the former pastor. Regardless of your relationship with the former pastor, remain positive and openly appreciative of the work he has done. Communicating the positive things you notice about the parish is an act of charity that you too will welcome from the pastor who eventually will replace you. This signals a positive tone to the entire parish, that you are a leader who affirms people's talents and gifts and who recognizes contributions. The outgoing pastor likely will give you greater cooperation if he sees you as friend rather than as critic. Every parish has unique gifts and virtues that comprise the legacy your predecessor leaves behind. Note and generously comment on these things.

Listen to the outgoing pastor. When you meet with the outgoing pastor, ask questions of fact and substance regarding money, staff, and procedure as well as subjective questions about his impact, major challenges, best moments, and current concerns. Then give him time to talk. Listen well and become a "student" to the outgoing pastor's "teacher," even if you have substantial differences with him. Building a connection with your brother priest makes you better informed and paves the way for consultations after your arrival. It also gives the outgoing pastor a better sense of who you are, inclining him to leave a more favorable impression of you during his final days as pastor.

Recap discussions. Whenever you meet with the outgoing pastor, begin with a short recap of the past meeting to ensure that you both are on the same page. Some meetings over meals might be useful, but meetings at his office may prove more helpful since there he can introduce you to staff, easily retrieve needed documents, show you keys and locks, and help you capture the feel of the parish. At times, for reasons of confidentiality, you may wish to meet off site so that you both are free to discuss sensitive concerns without being overheard or interrupted.

Handle resistance. Use all your powers of persuasion to induce the outgoing pastor to meet with you, even if it takes inviting him to join you at his favorite restaurant to get him to the table! However, if he refuses to meet with you, you may have to arrange meetings with his associate(s) or past associates. Preparation makes for better transitioning; don't allow the departing pastor's resistance to leave you uninformed or unprepared.

Anticipate special circumstances. If you are preparing to lead a parish currently without an active pastor, it is even more important to prepare yourself—and to engage with the people who await your arrival. If there is an assigned temporary administrator, that person is, of course, a critical referent. Resolve to measure that person's level of engagement in the daily life of the parish. (This role is anything but standardized even within one diocese. It could be the "next door" pastor, a staff member, a priest tapped from the ranks of retired priests, etc. He or she may be restricted to purely "administrative" duties or may be supplying a pastoral presence as well.) Ask this person about his or her insights about the community, the staff, the finances, the councils, the pastoral needs, and any special concerns that have developed since the parish has been without a full-time pastor. Next, consider who on the staff might help you understand the loss of the pastor, the days or months spent without a pastor, and any other situations pertinent to current parish life.

> I urge you therefore, brothers, by the mercies of God, to offer your bodies as a living sacrifice, holy and pleasing to God, your spiritual worship. Do not conform yourselves to this age but be transformed by the renewal of your mind, that you may discern what is the will of God, what is good and pleasing and perfect.
> *(Rom 12:1-2)*

Relating and Ministering to the New Parish Staff

All antennae are up during the pastor placement process. Sometimes the underground communication system within a parish will alert staff and parish members to news of a new pastor well ahead of any formal announcement. Staff and parishioners are just as interested in learning who the "new boss" will be as is the priest in learning what his new assignment will be, giving the lie to the sentiment of a priest who said with some agitation, "What are they worried about? *I'm* the one changing jobs, not them!"

Your change is everyone's change. It is a mark of respect and an act of charity to recognize that many lives will be affected by your arrival.

Predictable Concerns of Parish Staff

Staff concerns may not be grounded in reality, but until staff hears otherwise, their concerns *are* reality. Even those people who don't have anxieties of their own may be affected by others' worries. You may want to keep in mind the following essential points as you contemplate your relationship with your new staff.

Enter the world of the other.

Whether relating to staff, associate pastor, or parishioners, the new pastor must enter the mindset of the "other" so he can understand better, communicate more effectively, and exercise effective leadership.

Remember:

- Change (even welcome change) triggers worry and anxiety.

- When the pastor changes, everything changes.

- Staff departures are common when pastors change.

- People know that new pastors can alter job descriptions and eliminate jobs.

When people encounter things they don't understand or that were not fully explained to them, they seek meaning. Even before you set foot on the property, staff will be trying to understand the "meaning" of your being assigned to the parish! Your best strategy is to over-communicate. When you write and speak, do so with the listener in mind. Remember, where there is fear, misunderstanding abounds. Take time and be patient. Know it is your job to be personal and clear without being confrontational or judgmental. Keep in mind the Good Shepherd when you speak, write, or e-mail, especially when you feel under stress. In the absence of clear communication, staff may be tempted to fill in the blanks, thereby increasing the odds of misunderstanding.

Staff members' fears that they may be forced to change roles, accept new responsibilities, or even resign are not unreasonable. Many can point to precedents when friends and colleagues found themselves in similar situations. You have the authority to make responsible personnel changes, but you also have the responsibility to allay unnecessary fear and be clear about your expectations regarding each staff member. Clarity leads to cooperation and inspires confidence.

Some things will be beyond your control.

Regardless of your plans or intentions, there may be voluntary staff changes that you won't be able to prevent. You *can*, however, manage such changes and even use them positively for further momentum.

It is not unusual to experience voluntary staff resignations of up to a third of the staff roster regardless of the pastor selected, his management and leadership style, or the stability of the team. Change invites change.

Staff members who remain, however, may view voluntary change with suspicion. "What do they know that I don't?" is a common, often unvoiced concern of those left behind.

When a staff member announces a voluntary departure, consider the following:

Listen carefully and nonjudgmentally even if the person offers criticism. Showing respect is key. If the meeting is emotionally charged, remember that hostility is often a manifestation of fear. If you perceive hostility, look for the fear that grounds it. Listen empathically and use paraphrasing to signal your attentive listening. If you feel defensive, try taking notes as the person talks; doing so can give you breathing room and keep you focused on the person's ideas, rather than your own. When you listen well, people feel better and spread the word. Compassionate listening to those who are leaving may be rewarded by what they say about you when they go.

Respond with encouragement rather than advice. Supportive listening is the essence of effective pastoral counseling. If you're listening to a discouraging narrative about the parish history, pick out themes and offer feedback with a positive look to the future. If you hear insecurity over a decision, point out the courage it took to share that ambivalence. If you hear resentment and anger, comment on the person's forthrightness and strength. If you hear sadness and fear, assure them of your confidence in their finding the right path for themselves through further reflection and discernment. In short, as you listen, comment with confidence and offer encouragement.

> You who dwell in the shelter of the Most High,
> who abide in the shade of the Almighty,
> Say to the LORD,"My refuge and fortress,
> my God in whom I trust."
> He will rescue you from the fowler's snare,
> from the destroying plague,
> He will shelter you with his pinions,
> and under his wings you may take refuge;
> his faithfulness is a protecting shield.
> *(Ps 91:1-4)*

Secure the permission of those leaving regarding any parish-wide announcement about their departure. You may even craft the message with their help. It is important that parishioners and staff hear about any departures from you as well as from those leaving. Do this in a timely manner with no commentary on your part, other than your support and best wishes. This is not an opportunity for rebuttal.

Don't hold on when people leave. Let them go. Resist inviting them back for a party or a staff meeting. Once they have made the decision, it is best to let them depart as soon as possible. It is natural for departing staff to experience mixed feelings about their decision. Let them work out those feelings on their own in their new setting.

Just because you can does not mean that you should— just yet.

Leaders without followers are very, very lonely. We may know pastors who are "the boss" but who lead only themselves. Effective leaders use a number of strategies to make sure that staffs follow their lead. As you establish your relationship with your new staff, consider the following:

Spend your first 120 days interviewing and listening. Don't make the mistake of applying this principle only to parishioners. It goes for the staff as well. Even if you see glaring deficiencies or needs for change, resist taking action until people come to know you as a listening and understanding leader. "Being right" isn't enough. You must also take time to ensure you are perceived as wise. A wise bishop once remarked that his job was "not only to do the right thing but also to be *perceived* as doing the right thing." The 120 days go quickly, so interview methodically and persistently until you have gathered enough information to begin building on a solid foundation.

Resist the temptation to recruit your former staff. Though it is understandable to want to bring on someone who is known and trusted, doing so may create a near impossible situation for that person who may end up being viewed by current staff as "Father's favorite." Your former staff may have flourished because of the circumstances in that particular time and place. Embrace the opportunity to seek the new and to discover what may be.

Seek support when considering a staff removal. Don't go it alone. Check in early with the diocesan human resources department. It is likely there are policies and procedures in place to help both you and the staff person. Getting help early forestalls a litany of unproductive and painful incidents. Firing a staff member should always be a last resort. Retaining staff who are failing, however, leads to dysfunction. It is important to discern when immediate action is necessary for the overall health of the parish. Prayer and wise counsel will help overcome unnecessary conflict and help you do the right, if difficult, thing!

If you must terminate someone's employment, do so with firmness and respect. Firmness generates respect for you; respect demonstrates care for the other's integrity. Don't avoid doing the "hard stuff" if your heart tells you it's necessary; it is an essential part of leadership. Keep in mind that having a crucial conversation with a staff member may help the person find his or her real vocation in life. When you act, do not be seen as abrupt. Listen well. When you make the difficult decision, communicate it directly and clearly to the person, in person if at all possible.

Introducing Yourself

It's vital to put your best self forward when you meet parish staff for the first time. A warm and genuine self-introduction will go a long way to making a worthy first impression.

To start your introduction, you might consider hosting a joint lunch for the staffs of your current and new parishes. Make introductions and then leave folks to eat, enjoy, and talk on their own. Some pastors have found this to be a valuable strategy in making the transition from their old to their new staff.

It would be hard to overemphasize the importance of sensitivity in the way you talk about your old parish with the new staff. Whether you spin tales of wonder or of criticism, few really want to hear about it, even if they don't interrupt you! Save those stories for a golfing partner on your day off. (But beware: he may also have a truckload of stories!)

Interview each staff member of the new parish, regardless of rank, tenure, and full- or part-time status. During the interviews, your job is to let each person talk, to be approachable and friendly, and to begin learning patterns of behavior, standard operating procedures, and underlying assumptions. These conversations should lead to growth of staff confidence in their new leader.

Regarding these conversations, you will want to

- Schedule more than one over the first few months. This allows you to make the first session about getting to know the person and his or her concerns.

- Make a later meeting a time for reviewing what is in writing about his or her job or ministry description. If such documents do not exist, see the note below.

- Still later, perhaps toward the second half of your first year, help staff persons set goals and priorities that align with your own and with the parish mission. In doing so you send an implicit message that you value their work and that their contributions to the parish really matter.

- As mentioned earlier, interview even those who already have given notice. When interviewing someone who is leaving, even if a volunteer, your job is to listen, even through complaints, to hear the issues and learn what changes may be needed.

The First Year

Think of your first year in the new parish as the "getting to know you" year, almost a honeymoon during which you and others will decide together who does what, what needs to be done and when, who is best at certain tasks, and how you will handle day-to-day operations and ministry.

Some things you might want to do include:

Develop or update clear, specific, and accurate job descriptions. Don't be surprised if there are none in your new parish or that they may be outdated. If job descriptions need to be created or modified, enlist the support of each person in writing and refining his or her job description. There may be written guidance or resources and experts available from the diocese. You, of course, can have the final word, but asking everyone to describe what they do in writing helps secure buy-in and builds trust that you will need, particularly when you want to point toward new priorities and agenda. When you need to adjust a job description, do so with care and respect. Build succinct statements of key performance areas, naming critical responsibilities and expectations with quantifiable as well as qualifiable measurements of success. Avoid catch-all "laundry-lists" that diminish and distract from priorities.

Be careful to schedule and plan for time spent in meetings, especially as you start your new term. Staff will want meetings to be both productive and informative. A wise practice for you and staff is to solicit agenda items and share reports in writing or via e-mail prior to in-person meetings. This practice allows people to prepare for meetings and respond thoughtfully to questions and concerns. Make meetings important, valuable, and dynamic, clearly connecting agendas to planning and execution of goals. To gain everyone's sense of participation, try such methods as splitting a large staff into groups of two or three people, letting each group discuss a topic or concern and report to the larger group. Begin meetings with prayer to set a calm and congenial tone.

Avoid letting "talkers" dominate while others remain silent in large group meetings. Remember the differences between introverts and extroverts and allow introverts time to think before asking for group input or response. Allowing some people to dominate and others to feel unheard can sow seeds of resentment and misunderstanding. Get everyone involved; don't play favorites.

Host a retreat or day of recollection in the first year, usually after the first 120 days, when you'll have a clearer sense of the staff and parish needs. If feasible, hire a facilitator to lead the day so that you can relax, renew your own spirit, enjoy the experience, learn, and most important, engage on equal footing with your staff. Resolve with everyone to keep "business" out of discussion, a very difficult resolution to keep! Some staffs allow for short business check-ins when the retreat closes or before people go home or return to the parish.

Decide how you want staff and parishioners to address you and ask how they wish to be addressed. This may seem somewhat trivial, but it isn't. Will you be called "Monsignor" or "Father" or "Father (first name)" or just by your first name without a title? Staff and parishioners will also have preferences. Some want to be called by their first names, some by "Mrs. (last name)." It will be much easier for all if you are deferential and flexible.

Decide how you will handle exceptions, for instance, those who will not make the staff meetings, those who don't want to go on retreat, and so on. A parish policy manual makes handling these situations much easier. It is possible your new parish doesn't have a manual or has one that has been long neglected and unused; in that case, take the initiative and assign someone or a team to create or resurrect a useful manual. Remember though, policies establish the rule, but there may be valid and necessary exceptions. Your diocese or fellow pastors in other parishes may have a policy manual that you can adapt.

Work carefully with the parish business manager regarding finances. Even if you have "no head for figures," it is essential that you be aware of parish financial procedures and the current financial status. Ultimately, you are the one responsible for the money. When you understand the money situation, you can plan intelligently and work more effectively for the good of the parish. Work together with the business manager to review monthly and annual budgets. Transparency in financial matters is essential to the financial well-being of a parish. If there is no parish business manager, you will need to identify who handles finances and if that is a desirable situation.

Work closely with the principal and school committees if your parish has a school. Though Catholic schools take up much time and require many human and financial resources, they are not an adjunct to the parish but comprise an essential element of the parish mission and ministry. Your role as pastor encompasses the school in a very significant way and that role cannot be relegated to any other administrator. Relations between school and parish may get strained at times, but you must guard against an "us" versus "them" mentality. School and parish are one, and ultimately you are the leader. Enlist the principal as your ally and work with him or her to establish mutual support. Engage others to support you and the principal.

Support your ministerial staff by planning to visit their meetings, especially with their staff or volunteers. It's impossible to be everywhere that people in the parish want you to be. But it is vital that you build strategies to become informed and prepared. Learn names (use name tags and name "tents" if necessary). Follow up as needed using e-mail to coach, console, and collaborate. Remember, aside from Sunday, meetings may be some people's only connection with you, profoundly shaping their impression of you. The good word travels fast; discouraging words travel faster.

In some cases, an incoming pastor may get labeled or categorized before he has even met very many parishioners. Some parishioners may resist getting to know you and your style, preferring to rely on reputation, rumor, or first impressions. Staff can be important personal ambassadors! They often are the people who encourage parishioners to exercise charity and welcome the new pastor with open minds.

Relating to New Parishioners

Parishioners have expectations great and small, expressed and unexpressed, personal and general. Many parishioners will expect you to meet their needs and fulfill their hopes, regardless of what you want—and can do.

You bring to your new parish a myriad of approaches and resources. But what worked at one place may not work in another. Discussions with priests who successfully made the move to a new parish suggest that most parishioners really want from their pastor only four essential things:

1. **Trust.** This is the basic component of every relationship. Be consistently who you are so that everyone knows they can trust your word, your promise, and your vision.

2. **Time.** Your time is the greatest gift you can share. So safeguard your schedule. Being busy does not mean you are productive. Rushing and racing, late here, later there, are symptoms of an ineffective leader. People don't want leaders to be "busy"; they want them to be "effective." Don't do it all. Do what is needed "next."

3. **Talk.** Develop your verbal skills and invite conversations. Never use being an introvert as an excuse to dodge communicating. Let people know what's on your mind. When conflicts arise, don't shy away. Conflict can be healthy if you don't fear it. Conflict presents you with four alternatives: fight, flight, freeze, or figure it out. Being the new guy offers you the opportunity to approach conflict as a learner. Often, the best way to figure it out is to talk it out.

4. **Connection.** Connect with others often—through e-mail, phone calls, personal notes, and meetings. People respond positively when they know they are being listened to, affirmed and encouraged, or respected and acknowledged. Demonstrate your interest and concern.

Strategies for Leaving Your Current Parish

Relating to Current Parish Staff and Lay Leaders

Early in the transition process, even before the move, a newly-named pastor will naturally begin to focus some attention on his new parish. But until he officially leaves his current assignment, he will remain an important part of the transition process for that parish as well. It's easy to forget about this reality and tempting to avoid its demands. During this period the pastor straddles two worlds.

Throughout the transition period, an outgoing pastor should meet with his current staff to discuss fears and anxieties and to foster hopes and dreams for the future of the parish. The staff should use this time to sort out their own personal feelings and to support one another. The transition period offers an opportunity for informal parish evaluation: What do we do well as a faith community? What are our strengths? Where would we like to do better?

The attitude of the parish staff often sets the tone for the rest of the parish community. Parishioners will be less anxious during the transition process if they see the staff remaining positive and hopeful about the future. Current staff and parish leaders need to remain in the loop with you during these days, keeping their fingers on the pulse of the parish. They can help you determine what should be shared with the entire parish community and what information should be passed on to the incoming pastor. Encourage staff and parish leaders to set aside significant private and communal time to pray for everyone involved in and affected by the transition. That prayer is likely to lead to joined planning, for example, how to say good-bye to the current pastor, how to welcome the new pastor, how to celebrate Sunday liturgy with both priests as concelebrants.

The exiting pastor, perhaps with the help of a facilitator, may decide to convene his current staff to discuss how the parish will prepare for and welcome their new pastor. Together they might discuss upcoming events to which the incoming pastor should be invited, such as a parish pastoral council meeting, a parish social event, or a Sunday Eucharist.

When an Associate Is Named Pastor of His Current Parish

When the associate pastor is named the new pastor, parishioners and staff may express less uncertainty, since the associate is known to them. If this is your situation, don't absent yourself from the exercises and activities that other new pastors need to engage in. There may still be matters for which you and other people are unprepared. The mantle of leadership may draw out previously inexperienced attitudes, convictions, and behaviors from those who are staff members or parishioners.

During your first year, you and staff members—whether you had been friends, colleagues, or even had moments of conflict—will need to forge new respectful working relationships, that is, new boundaries and rules of engagement. As the new pastor, you now act as supervisor of people for whom you may not have had oversight. A good practice might be to begin with formal review of role descriptions suggested previously. (See "The First Year" on page 27.) Such conversations give each of you a chance to experience the reformed relationships.

Mostly, in less intense ways, the process of renegotiating is also important for at least some parishioners. Parishioners need to recognize that you are now in a role that brings more responsibilities and a different perspective on things.

Making a Clean Exit

When leaving a pastorate, say your good-byes and then stay away as much as possible for a respectful period of time. The new pastor won't stand a chance if you show up at bingo, graduation, and the Spring Fling. Find reasons not to attend, and be happy the former pastor of *your* new parish is doing the same! This caution also applies to funerals and weddings—unless the new pastor agrees and is enthusiastic in his agreement, and the two of you work out any details together. These are good discussion points to address, if possible, before you each move. As the old country and western song asks, "How Can I Miss You If You Won't Go Away?"

> I command you: be strong and steadfast! Do not fear nor be dismayed, for the LORD, your God, is with you wherever you go.
>
> *(Josh 1:9)*

At your final meeting with current staff, affirm each and every individual in a way he or she won't forget. Be sincere, speaking from your heart as well as your head. Make sure each person feels affirmed. But be careful of your humor here. If you make comments sweet rather than sarcastic, the good taste will linger longer.

If you receive good-bye gifts, send handwritten thank-you notes within one month. Yes, people notice. No, they won't tell you they noticed.

The Skill of Planned Transition

Successful transition requires thought and planning. Ten questions you should ponder during transition include:

1. How do I feel about leaving/going/transitioning? (Ponder quietly or in a journal.)

2. When have I successfully transitioned, and what did I do well? (Focus only on your strengths and accomplishments, and don't be shy or modest.)

3. What support do I personally need as I make this move? (What, who, when, where?)

4. What am I called to accomplish in my interior life at this time? (Talk with your spiritual director.)

5. Where do I need to be most careful: in my tendencies, my assumptions, my bad habits? (Pick only a few of the big ones!)

6. What is the history of my new parish? (Google it! Ask around.)

7. What do I know and like about the parish neighborhood? Do I understand its people and their needs? (Drive it and walk it with someone knowledgeable about the community. Work to see it with the eyes of a traveler. Robert Louis Stevenson once said: "There are no foreign lands. It is the traveler only who is foreign.")

8. What do I know about the pastor I am succeeding? (Regardless of what others have said, how can I remain open and contribute to making this a smooth transition for him and me?)

9. What are the most important aspects of parish life that I want to discuss with the exiting pastor? (Ask this question early and often and reflect on your ability and willingness to respond to what you learn.)

10. As the process moves forward, what do I notice about myself? (Keep a keen eye on your feelings, their flow and their movement from day to day. Be honest with yourself.)

> But he with an oath, through the one who said to him:
> "The Lord has sworn, and he will not repent:
> 'You are a priest forever.'"
> *(Heb 7:21)*

Organizational Aspects to Remember

Remember the dos and don'ts of new pastors, and recognize the needs and expectations of your new parishioners. Your role for the first 120 days is that of observer, summarizer, and interested inquirer. But your role is not all passive, for simultaneously you must begin sharing your vision for the parish. Approach every situation with confidence and tranquility. Your attitude toward what you encounter will be important—and it will be noticed.

Learn the parish culture, quickly. How are decisions made, who takes initiative, who seem to be the people at the edges? What does the state of the physical plant say about the place? How do people interact on Sunday, at meetings, during choir rehearsal, at parish events? Do the rectory, office, and grounds look welcoming?

Make changes with a clear purpose in mind. You will enjoy a bit of a honeymoon period during which you can make small changes at your discretion. But be careful not to make all changes that way. Be aware that the flags, songs, rituals, statues, and so on, that may be anathema to you are very important to someone in the parish. Seek advice. When there is no clear opposition, change as you see fit, but be attentive to the results!

Evaluate your staff with firmness and friendliness. Take a good, long, careful, and prayerful look at the staff. Always affirm any sign of cooperation. Be conscious of those who see themselves in privileged positions. If someone routinely ignores you and your direction, you need to speak with that person. Hold the person accountable, and set up a way that you can be accountable in return. When you find yourself struggling, it is usually best to seek advice outside the parish. Some pastors employ an executive coach or a mentor. It can be very helpful to seek advice from the appropriate diocesan agency and the human resources office. There might be a priests' group that you can consult or join for support and information.

Master the budget. There is power in commas and decimal points. It is *essential* you understand the budget. You will have to be aware of what money comes in, what goes out, where it is spent, and by whom. Ultimately, the consequences of all those decisions rest on your shoulders. Be sensitive about potentially expensive changes you hope to make, *especially to the rectory.* You have every right to a nice home. You may not have every right to a wine cellar!

Learn names early, including children's and teens'. Recognize key players. Acknowledging the importance of everyone's contribution is key to becoming an effective pastor early on. You will enjoy celebrity status for a while, but soon enough you will be known for the gifts you bring and the quality of your personal interactions.

Seek to resolve any ongoing problems. Ask for input from all who are affected by them. Be cautious of uncovering too much history and especially careful about attributing blame. Rather, focus staff and parishioners toward the future; work together to address the identified issues and establish any necessary policies or procedures to ensure they do not recur. Assigning blame stifles initiative; problem solving done cooperatively motivates. Don't contribute to the "problem pool" by acting too quickly or unilaterally. Remember that giving people a sense of ownership with you goes a long way toward bringing about positive change.

Make a solid first impression. Seize the first 120 days and realize they hold the key to a smooth transition. If the old adage is true that "You're always smarter than your predecessor (and dumber than your successor)," you'll have an opportunity to seize when you first arrive at your new parish. Plan carefully during the months and weeks prior to moving to your new assignment. Brainstorm, remember, dream, research, read, pray, and devote time to planning for those critical 120 days. If those four months go well, you'll be off to a great start and on a trajectory to successful ministry.

Maintain balance. Commit yourself early to a balanced lifestyle. Your day off, how you spend your time, where you are seen, what you will and will not do are all determinants of healthy living and effective ministry. The parish can be a major part of your life without consuming all of it. Delegate. Rely on your staff and associates even if they won't do things exactly as you would. Apply this significant piece of wisdom offered by psychiatrist Dr. Rudolf Dreikurs: "Remember, we teach responsibility by giving responsibility." Find ways to give everyone on the staff a chance to grow by delegating early and often.

Most of all, pray. Keep your focus. While much of the transition process involves nuts-and-bolts issues, it must be deeply rooted in the theology and spirituality of call and response. While you will need your budget, your staff, your meetings, your human relations skills, and your instincts to succeed, you must also stay grounded in prayer. As you learned long ago, serious prayer requires a certain minimum of alone-time in addition to community celebration. Remember that special priest you knew and admired who was prayerful?

> Remember not the events of the past,
> the things of long ago consider not;
> See, I am doing something new!
> Now it springs forth, do you not perceive it?
> *(Isa 43:18-19a)*

What Doesn't Work (or "How to Fail Even Before You Begin")

The pastor's attitude is of critical importance during the transition process. The following are negative attitudes and behaviors known to hinder smooth transitions, followed by more helpful, positive behaviors:

Negative Attitudes

- "I want to be liked." Wanting to be accepted and loved so much that you can never say "no" to anyone.

- "It's my parish, I can do what I want." Doing your own thing no matter what and failing to consult with people who are affected or who must support your move.

- "It is just a job change." Forgetting it's a ministry and lacking real investment in any ministerial assignment. Doing only what you have to do. Moving on with ease because you failed to establish and build relationships.

- "I don't want to be there." Not looking forward to the new parish and dwelling on negative expectations of what lies ahead; avoiding the hard work of transition that could promote healing and growth.

- "All this talk about keeping an open mind is for the birds!" Assuming you already know what is needed and expecting the people to adjust, not you. After all, you're their new pastor.

Negative Behaviors

- Not meeting the new parish until the first day, but remaining focused on your current parish instead, doing nothing with the new parish before you arrive. This failure to plan ahead may indicate you are not ready to let go of the parish you are leaving.

- Making staff changes prior to, or immediately upon arrival. Though usually an attempt to avoid conflict, this poor strategy inevitably creates worse and longer-lasting conflict.

- Bringing old staff along to the new parish. This two-edged sword preemptively eliminates staff at the new parish and simultaneously creates vacancies in the staff of the previous parish.

- Neither listening nor asking good questions. Making decisions based on impulse or personal conviction without looking at data or collaborating with others before making decisions. You may end up saying "yes" to everything or "no" to everything; either way, your decisions won't reflect careful consideration of potential consequences.

Positive Behavior

- Collaboration, careful listening, and asking good questions. The naysayers will give their opinions, but they need not prevail. The effective pastor considers the entire parish community when making decisions. Special-interest groups will lobby for their agendas, but the pastor shepherds the entire community. When he makes a mistake, he will admit it and move on.

- Listen, ask, and pray whenever controversy arises. When things go well, be relentless in discovering those responsible for the good work. Thank and affirm them often!

- Express gratitude for being where you are. Be welcoming to be welcomed. "This is really an easy job," said a newly assigned bishop. "I look at people and I smile, then they cry and thank me."

Conclusion

This guide was developed for transitioning pastors in the hope that the resources of theology, psychology, spirituality, and missiology will be brought to bear on every experience of pastoral change.

Of course, few transitions go perfectly. Some outgoing pastors do not see the need for the kind of preparations endorsed here. Tragically, they may expect to say what was said to them: "Here are the keys." We hope these pages have made clear that for the sake of pastors and parishioners, and for the sake of the mission, such scenarios must be avoided!

This booklet was cowritten by pastors who have recently transitioned to new parishes and by professionals who consulted with them. We sincerely hope *A Priest's Guide* will become a well-used resource that helps priests understand the processes going on inside them and within both their parishes—the current and the new.

We encourage you to refer to these pages prior to communicating your wants and needs in your new parish, and to let this resource guide your dialogue with those you will leave behind and those you will soon embrace.

Note that two guides accompany this priest's guide: one written for parish staff persons and one for parishioners, each of whom who will experience this important time of transition in unique ways. It could be very helpful to encourage their reading and discussion of the guides as changes are planned and unfold.

May you be richly blessed during your time of transition and in your new ministry!

Appendix

Administrative Interview Questionnaire

As a new or newly-appointed pastor, plan to address the following questions through personal interviews, group discussions with staff, and careful reading of parish policy and procedural manuals.

Develop clearly written and detailed responses wherever possible. Such efforts will yield practical information about many aspects of parish operation and a broad knowledge base that will inform the early days of your ministry in the new parish.

Remember to always end interviews by summarizing, using declarative sentences to express what you heard—even if you don't agree with it. This will help correct any misunderstanding and communicate not only *what* you heard but, more important, *that* you heard. It can result in your greatest "PR" outcome: "He listens!"

The following sets of questions are examples of questions pastors have asked or wish they had asked. These sample questions are grouped according to broad areas of parish life and should help you select your own issues of inquiry.

While these lists may at first appear quite extensive, you are sure to identify new questions. Be selective with the list, and add your own concerns. Stick to a short list of three to five questions in individual interviews, but end every interview by asking, "What did I forget to ask? Is there anything else you'd like to add?"

Mission, Vision, Values

- Is there a statement of parish mission, and how is it used? When was it written? How often is it reviewed and revised?

- How are parishioner leaders and new staff oriented to the parish mission, vision, and values?

- How are mission and values and vision statements shared with parishioners?

- Is there a strategic or long-range plan in place? How do the principal ministries relate to mission and plan? Who created the current strategic or long-range plan? When was the plan created? How often is it reviewed and revised?

- Are there any language or cultural needs the parish should consider, now or later?

Standard Operating Procedures

- How have decisions been made here? What processes have been used and who has been consulted?

- How is the Sunday bulletin prepared and published?

- Who has keys to which facilities?

- How detailed are the parishioner enrollment files? How are they updated—by counts or surveys?

- Who makes entries into the sacramental records? What is electronic and what is recorded manually?

- What is the procedure when something needs to be purchased or repaired?

- If there is a parish staff or other leadership groups, do they meet? If so, when and where and how often? Who prepares and communicates the agenda for the meeting?

- Who prepares the Mass schedule, and how is it made?

- Is there a committee that prepares liturgy and plans the liturgical seasons? How is liturgical music selected and by whom? (See more liturgy questions below.)

- How does the pastor's day off affect the schedule of meetings and Masses?

- Is there a list of passwords for computers and the security system? Who has them? Should they be changed? How are electronic files backed up? Who is responsible for technology (computer, Wi-Fi, networking, and so on)?

Councils and Commissions

- What councils, boards, commissions, and committees are actually up and running? In particular, are there a parish pastoral council and a finance council? (In some parishes they exist in name only; in others they function well. In most cases, they are mandated by canon law and/or diocesan policy. You may need to consult diocesan agencies for such policies and template documents that guide establishing and governing such councils.)

- Besides the parish staff, with whom should the new pastor meet and to whom should he listen? (Draw tight parameters here; this easily can become a long list. In a large parish, consider building a strategic schedule with assistance from parish council and staff.)

Personnel

- Are the personnel files up to date?

- Is any current parish employee considering leaving or retiring?

- How are days off and vacation scheduled and approved?

- Are there priests who assist on weekends or when the pastor or other priest is on vacation? How do parishioners respond to them?

- Does the pastor have his own administrative assistant?

- If the former pastor has retired and continues to live in the rectory or on the parish campus, how will the staff be reoriented to no longer see him as their "boss"?

- Are staff, key volunteers, and teachers in compliance with policies for protection of children and youth?

- Are there accurate and current job descriptions for every staff member? Does each staff member have a copy of his or her job description?

- How often are performance reviews scheduled? Who conducts them?

- What was the leadership style of the previous pastor and how would it compare with your own?

Buildings and Maintenance

- Who opens/closes the church on what days?

- Which buildings need significant repairs or renovation? Is there a fund or budget for these repairs?

- How are the facilities of the parish used and who schedules them?

- Is there a list of preferred vendors for plumbing, electrical, heating services, and emergency contacts?

- Where are heating and air conditioning units located? Who is authorized to operate them? Are there quick-reference guides at each location giving clear directions for operation?

- What kinds of routine plant maintenance go on throughout the year, weekly, monthly, seasonally? Who coordinates? Is there an operations manual and a way to document maintenance performances and inspections?

- Where are nearest fire and police stations? Are there emergency procedures for fire, water damage, health emergencies, evacuations, and so on? Who creates these procedures and how often are they reviewed and updated?

Education

- If there is a school, what has been the history of the pastor's relationship to it?
- What has been the relationship of the pastor to the religious education program?
- What has been the relationship between the school and the religious education program?
- Do the programs we have address all ages, and do they convey clear, authentic, and compelling expressions of the Church's faith?
- Are teachers and catechists well-prepared to teach the Catholic faith? Do teachers and catechists (volunteer and paid) have proper certifications?
- Is everyone who works with children in compliance with diocesan policies on the protection of children and youth?

Liturgy and Sacraments

- What are the liturgical ministries and who leads and participates?
- Who attends Mass, are any trends in participation apparent, who's missing?
- How are the parish's children and young people involved in liturgy?
- How is the RCIA implemented throughout the year? Evangelization?
- What special occasions during the year have a significant liturgical component?
- What devotional celebrations take place?

- Are there any scheduled or upcoming significant parish celebrations, such as anniversaries, dedications of facility, and so on?

- How many weddings, funerals, and baptisms occur on average annually? Who handles these liturgies and preparation programs?

Social Outreach

- What service and advocacy ministries are offered here?

- Is there a relationship with another parish community in the diocese or elsewhere in the world?

- Does pastor or parish have ecumenical relationships with nearby pastors, congregations, temples, or mosques?

- What does the parish do to serve the wider community?

- How does the parish express Catholic social teaching and work for justice, nonviolence, and peace?

- How do young people become involved in service and outreach?

Finance

- Are our financial practices consistent with diocesan policies and guidelines? What still needs to be implemented?

- What is the true financial situation in the parish? Has it been reported accurately to the diocese and the parishioners?

- What is the community's understanding of stewardship, and how is it expressed?

- Who oversees parish finances—a business manager, a parish accountant, a volunteer, or the pastor? What is the state of the parish finance council?

- Are there ways that money is collected, raised, spent, or given away that may be unique to this parish?

- Who makes purchases for the parish? Who is issued a purchase card or credit card?

- Who is authorized to sign checks?

- How many parish accounts are there, and is the pastor a signatory on each of them? If not, why not? Who makes bank deposits?

- Who collects and counts money at Masses and at parish events? What money handling procedures are in place? Are background checks done on people who handle money and manage accounts? Where are cash and checks stored prior to bank deposit?

- Who receives stipends, remunerations, gifts, bonuses during the year? What amounts and what rationales support the practices?

- Who pays for the pastor's cell phone and, if installed, private line?

- Who pays for premium cable television, personal web access, and food and beverages, including alcohol?

- How are personnel paid (by parish check or by a payroll vendor), and how often (weekly, semi-monthly, monthly)? Who distributes paychecks?

Miscellaneous

- What have been painful issues in the parish's history?

- How tech-savvy is the parish staff and the parish office? Do either need updating? Who prepares meals and purchases food for those living in the rectory? Is there a cook? Is there an expectation that staff members and the pastor eat certain meals together? Does anyone dining regularly in the rectory have food allergies?

- Are there defined common and private areas in the rectory and are these areas respected?

- Have pets been allowed in the rectory and/or office? Are any staff members allergic to pets?

- What is the policy regarding smoking on parish grounds and in parish buildings, including the rectory?

- Do the rectory and other buildings have, or will they need to have, accommodations for physical disabilities?